Meredith® Books
Des Moines, Iowa

© Copyright 1998 Kraft Foods, Inc.—recipes and food photographs.
© Copyright 1998 Meredith Corporation—text and lifestyle photographs.
All rights reserved. Printed in the United States of America.
Printing Number and Year: 5 4 3 2 1   03 02 01 00 99
Library of Congress Catalog Card Number: 98-68024
ISBN: 0-696-20901-2 Canadian BN: 12348 2887 RT

For more food ideas visit our
Web site at www.kraftfoods.com

Credits

Editorial and Design:
Meredith Integrated Marketing

Recipe Development and Testing:
Kraft Kitchens

Food Styling:
Amy Andrews, Elaine Funk, Bonnie
Rabert, Carol Parik, Judy Vance,
Karyn Wexler

Photography:
Jose Pascual, Joe Polivka, Steve Stitgen

Prop Styling:
Bonnie Kaplan, Kathy Lapin

Illustrator:
Jim Swanson

Produced by:
Meredith Books and Meredith
Integrated Marketing, 1716 Locust
Street, Des Moines, IA 50309-3023.

Meredith® Books
Editor: Chuck Smothermon
Design Production: Craig Hanken
Proofreader: Susie Kling
Production Director: Douglas M. Johnston

Editor in Chief: James D. Blume
Design Director: Matt Strelecki
Managing Editor: Gregory H. Kayko

Director, Sales & Marketing, Retail:
Michael A. Peterson
Director, Sales & Marketing,
Special Markets: Rita McMullen
Director, Operations: George A. Susral

Vice President, General Manager:
Jamie L. Martin

Happy Halloween
from the Kraft Kitchens!

Halloween is the holiday that most indulges
the imagination and invites the outrageous.
Best of all, it's not just for kids anymore,
it's for all of us. It has become the perfect
family holiday when parents and children
spend time together carving pumpkins,
creating costumes and planning parties.
And this year, the Kraft Kitchens joins in the
festivities by sharing some imaginative food
ideas, ghostly games and frightfully fun
decorating ideas with you. Plus, we have
put together practical tips that will help
you gear up for unforgettable parties
and seasonal activities.

We've tested all of the Halloween food ideas
in the Kraft Kitchens, so they're guaranteed
to put a smile on the face of every ghost
and goblin—plus the simple decorating
tips will make your home spooky, without
breaking your budget. So, as the bewitching
day approaches, rely on the Kraft Kitchens
for a howling great time.

Stephanie Williams

Stephanie Williams, Director, Kraft Kitchens

**Pictured on front cover: Ghosts in
the Graveyard (recipe, page 18)**

13 Tips for HALLOWEEN

Cap off the fall season by having a ghoulishly delightful Halloween get-together for family and friends. It's easy to make your party simple, yet full of fun, by following these 13 helpful hints.

About two weeks ahead, pick the date, time and theme for your Halloween party; make your guest list. Because a party, especially one for small children, can involve a lot of steps, don't try to do it all by yourself. Consider enlisting the help of other parents or hire a couple of teenagers.

Set the mood of your event with the invitations. You can purchase them or make your own. For a bewitching idea, use color-changeable markers and write your invitation on white paper, using the white marker (the words will be invisible). Then send each invitation in a heavy envelope with a color-changing marker. Include instructions to color the entire invitation—the words will appear like magic. For another idea, send your guests invitations written on masks. Simply buy inexpensive paper eye masks and write the words on the backs.

 Ten days before the party, address and mail or hand deliver the invitations. Don't forget to ask for an RSVP so you know how many guests will be coming!

A party wouldn't be a party without lots of good eats. Look through this book and  plan your menu. Make a shopping list of the ingredients you need to buy. Be sure to include film or buy a couple of disposable cameras, so you can place them around the room and let guests share in the pleasure of capturing the moments of fun.

Easy Table Decorations

When it comes to decorating the table for your Halloween party, natural materials such as gourds or miniature pumpkins, dried leaves, flowers or grasses make beautiful, yet inexpensive, accents. If you like, take the family on an outdoor excursion to look for colorful leaves or grasses to dry. You'll find gourds and miniature pumpkins at your supermarket or farmer's market.

 Buy your pumpkins early, while the selection is still good. Look for a variety of sizes and shapes for making different jack-o'-lanterns with interesting faces. Also, pick up some miniature pumpkins—they'll make great decorations and party favors.

As part of the party planning, buy or make costumes for your family. For costume ideas and trick-or-treat safety tips, see pages 29, 60 and 67.

Spooky Story Time

Take a few minutes to read some Halloween stories to your children. Be sure to select stories that are age-appropriate. Make the tales even more fun by adding your own scary or silly sound effects.

Have the youngsters help choose games and activities for your party.  Be sure to have some extra activities, in case a game you're expecting to last 45 minutes only lasts 15 minutes. If you like, make trick-or-treating or other Halloween activities part of the party fun. For example, you may want to plan an outing to one of the haunted houses in your area or to a mall. Most larger shopping malls offer parties or trick-or-treating for little ones on Halloween.

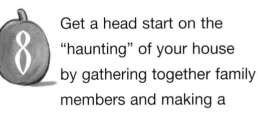 Get a head start on the "haunting" of your house by gathering together family members and making a special tape of spooky sounds. Also, remember to make or buy the decorations you'll need.

Make or buy party favors so each guest has a treat or gift to take home.

Party Favor Pizzazz

Party favors add an extra element of fun to any Halloween gathering. Favors needn't be elaborate or costly. They can be as simple as a small plastic toy or a Halloween lollipop. Or, make individual bundles of one of the snack mixes found in this book. Festively package the mix by encasing it in plastic wrap and tying each bundle with black curling ribbon. Be sure to make the bundles only a day or two ahead, so they stay fresh. If you have an instant camera, take snapshots of the costumed kids as take-home keepsakes.

10 Inject some Halloween fun into an ordinary afternoon by asking your kids to invite a few friends over after school to help make treats for the party. Let the kids mix up Trick or Treat Snack Mix, Candy Corn Popcorn Balls or even some Pumpkin Cupcakes (see recipes, pages 64, 63 and 22).

11 Two or three days ahead of the party, shop for groceries and any other items that you may need. If you're having a scary party, make some creepy-crawly ice cubes. Just fill an ice cube tray with prepared KOOL-AID Soft Drink Mix and add a gummy worm or candy bug to each cube, then freeze until solid. Kids will love the surprises in their drinks.

12 The day before the party, begin preparing the food. Carve the pumpkins—double check to make sure you have enough candles for the pumpkins or plan to use small flashlights, so you don't have to worry about potential accidents.

Block Party Fun

If you're looking for a unique neighborhood party, consider getting together with a few families on your block for a scarecrow-making party. Send out invitations instructing guests to bring old clothes for their scarecrows to wear and pumpkins for the heads; you supply the straw. After the creations are made and perched on front steps, head inside for a potluck dinner.

Creative Carving

Here are a few general hints for pumpkin carving:

- Draw a face on the pumpkin with markers before you start to carve.
- Cut the top of the pumpkin off at an angle, so the top won't fall through when the heat of the candle starts to shrivel up the pumpkin. Or, don't even cut the top off! Just cut out a hole in the back, scoop out the seeds and slide the candle through the hole.
- To keep the candle standing up straight, secure it in melted wax on a jar lid.
- If you like, carve several jack-o'-lanterns and group them together—it'll be more dramatic than just one pumpkin.
- If carving isn't your style, paint the jack-o'-lanterns instead (tip, page 51).

Before party day, finish making the food and hanging the decorations. Put out the disposable cameras or assign a couple of your helpers to be photographers and encourage them to take lots of photos. When party time comes, get involved and participate in as many activities as you can. Enjoy!

a bewitching

PARTY

There is no trick to putting together this Halloween celebration for ghosts and goblins of all ages. A holiday as fun as Halloween deserves food and drink full of glee—and this collection is bound to get laughs as well as compliments. You'll also find great tips for creating a haunted house and setting the mood for a party that's frightening, festive and fun.

Pumpkin Cupcakes (recipe, page 22)

VELVEETA® Salsa Dip

Tortilla chips, broccoli and cauliflower flowerets, pepper strips and baby-cut carrots all make great dunkers for this quick-to-fix party favorite.

Prep time: 5 minutes
Microwave time: 5 minutes

1   pound (16 ounces) VELVEETA
    Prepared Cheese Product,
    cut up
1   cup TACO BELL
    HOME ORIGINALS
    Thick 'N Chunky Salsa

Microwave prepared cheese product and salsa in 1½-quart microwavable bowl on HIGH 5 minutes or until prepared cheese product is melted, stirring after 3 minutes.

Serve hot with assorted tortilla chips.

Garnish with green and orange pepper cut-outs.

Makes 3 cups.

VELVEETA® Cheesy Chili Dip:
Substitute 1 can (15 ounces) chili for salsa. Serve hot with tortilla chips, French bread chunks and corn bread sticks.

Makes 3¾ cups.

TACO BELL and HOME ORIGINALS are trademarks owned and licensed by Taco Bell Corp.

VELVEETA® Salsa Dip

Cheezy Beer Dip

Cheezy Beer Dip

Keep a jar of CHEEZ WHIZ and a bottle of beer in your cupboard and, in just minutes, you can serve unexpected guests this delicious dip.

Prep time: 5 minutes
Microwave time: 2 minutes

1   jar (16 ounces) CHEEZ WHIZ
    Pasteurized Process Cheese
    Sauce
⅓ cup beer

Microwave process cheese sauce as directed on label.

Mix process cheese sauce and beer in bowl, stirring until mixture becomes smooth. Garnish with sliced green onion. Serve with pretzels, bread sticks or green onions.

Makes 2 cups.

Grilled Turkey Club

Grill it up, stack it high and let party-goers dig in—everyone is sure to relish this hearty meat-and-cheese sandwich.

Prep time: 5 minutes
Cooking time: 10 minutes

2   slices bread
2   KRAFT Singles Pasteurized
    Process Cheese Food
    Tomato slices
4   slices LOUIS RICH
    CARVING BOARD Thin Carved
    Oven Roasted Turkey Breast
2   slices OSCAR MAYER Bacon,
    crisply cooked
    Butter *or* margarine, softened

Top 1 bread slice with 1 process cheese food slice, tomato, turkey, bacon, second process cheese food slice and second bread slice.

Spread outside of sandwich with butter.

Cook in skillet on medium heat until lightly browned on both sides. Cut into triangles. Secure with toothpicks, if desired.

Makes 1 sandwich.

Scary Sounds

Scary noises turn an ordinary house into a haunted one. You can purchase special Halloween tapes, but it's more fun to gather the family around a tape recorder and use some ordinary household items to create your own personalized spooky soundtrack. Here are some ways to make scary sounds:

Breaking bones: Snap carrots in half.

Creaking hinge: Open and close a squeaky door or gate hinge.

Howling wind: Blow hard into the microphone.

Knocking: Knock on a piece of wood.

Rain: Pour uncooked rice into a metal pan.

Rattling bones: Shake dried elbow macaroni strung on a string.

Rattling chains: Shake a chain.

Thunder: Roll a rock around in a box.

Walking: Make clopping sounds with shoes on a table.

Grilled Turkey Club

a bewitching PARTY

Spooky Eyeball Tacos

Tasty meatballs are the eyeballs in this kid-pleasing dish.

Prep time: 15 minutes
Baking time: 20 minutes

1   **pound ground beef**
1   **package (10¾ ounces)**
      TACO BELL HOME ORIGINALS
      Taco Dinner Kit
      Shredded lettuce
      Chopped tomatoes
      BREAKSTONE'S *or* **KNUDSEN**
      Sour Cream

Mix meat and Seasoning Mix. Shape into 36 (1-inch) balls; place in 13x9-inch baking dish. Bake at 350°F for 15 to 20 minutes or until cooked through.

Fill each of 12 Taco Shells with 1 meatball, Taco Sauce, lettuce and tomato.

Top with 2 additional meatballs dipped in sour cream. Garnish with sliced pitted ripe olives to create "eyes."

Makes 12 servings.

Make-ahead tip: The meatballs can be made ahead and frozen in a zipper-style plastic freezer bag. To reheat, open bag slightly; microwave on HIGH 2 minutes.

TACO BELL and HOME ORIGINALS are trademarks owned and licensed by Taco Bell Corp.

Spooky Eyeball Tacos

Cheese 'N Fruit Kabobs

Making this snack is a perfect after-school activity—kids will have fun both threading and eating the kabobs. On short metal or wooden skewers, thread KRAFT Colby or Monterey Jack Cheese Cubes and pieces of assorted fresh fruit, such as grapes, strawberries, pineapple, apple or banana. Serve with strawberry preserves or grape jelly for dipping, if desired.

Cheese 'N Fruit Kabobs and Devilishly Delicious Snacks

Devilishly Delicious Snacks

Keep hungry Halloween revelers happy with this quick-to-put-together snack. Spread PHILADELPHIA FLAVORS Cheesecake Flavor Cream Cheese Spread on cinnamon or plain graham crackers or vanilla wafer cookies. Decorate with Halloween sprinkles, if desired.

Ghosts in the Graveyard

Eek! It's a party dessert that will disappear so quickly it's scary.

And the best part? You can prepare it several hours ahead (photo, front cover).

Prep time: 10 minutes plus refrigerating

1 package (16 ounces) chocolate sandwich cookies
3½ cups cold milk
2 packages (4-serving size *each*) JELL-O Chocolate Flavor Instant Pudding & Pie Filling
1 tub (12 ounces) COOL WHIP Whipped Topping, thawed

Crush cookies in zipper-style plastic bag with rolling pin or in food processor.

Pour cold milk into large bowl. Add pudding mixes. Beat with wire whisk 2 minutes. Gently stir in 3 cups of the whipped topping and ½ of the crushed cookies. Spoon into 13x9-inch dish. Sprinkle with remaining crushed cookies.

Refrigerate 1 hour or until ready to serve. Store leftover dessert, covered, in refrigerator.

Makes 15 to 18 servings.

To Decorate Graveyard: Decorate assorted cookies with decorating icings or gels to create "tombstones." Stand "tombstones" on top of dessert with candy corn, candy pumpkins and tiny jelly beans. Drop remaining whipped topping by spoonfuls onto dessert to create ghosts. Decorate with candies to create "eyes."

Boo Cups (photo, opposite page):
Layer pudding mixture, remaining crushed cookies and candy corn or tiny jelly beans in 12 to 16 glasses or clear plastic cups. Decorate with additional candies, decorated cookies and whipped topping, as desired.

Makes 12 to 16 servings.

Cool Ghoul Treats

Add a startling touch to your Halloween punch by chilling it with frozen "hands" made with prepared KOOL-AID Soft Drink Mix (any flavor) and clear plastic or latex gloves. If the gloves have a powdery residue inside, turn them inside out and soak in warm water or wipe with soapy water and rinse. Allow gloves to dry. Put a few gummy worms in gloves, if desired. Add enough soft drink to fill gloves, but not so full that the fingers will not move. Fasten gloves tightly with twist-ties. Place paper towels on a cookie sheet and lay "hands" on paper towels. Freeze. When frozen solid, carefully use scissors to cut gloves off frozen "hands." Float "hands" in bowl of punch.

Boo Cups (recipe, opposite page)

Creepy Crawly Gelatin

Garnish this easy-to-make mold with gummy worms galore.

Prep time: 10 minutes
Refrigerating time: 3½ hours

1½ cups boiling water
1 package (8-serving size)
    or 2 packages (4-serving size
    each) JELL-O Orange Flavor
    Gelatin Dessert
1½ cups cold water
    Gummy worms

Stir boiling water into gelatin in large bowl at least 2 minutes until completely dissolved. Stir in cold water. Pour into 9-inch pie plate which has been sprayed with no stick cooking spray.

Refrigerate about 1½ hours or until thickened (spoon drawn through leaves definite impression). Push gummy worms into gelatin. Refrigerate 2 hours or until firm. Unmold. Garnish with additional gummy worms, if desired.

Makes 8 servings.

Note: *To unmold,* dip pie plate in warm water for about 15 seconds. Gently pull gelatin from around edge with moist fingers. Place moistened serving plate on top of pie plate. Invert pie plate and serving plate; holding plates together, shake slightly to loosen. Gently remove pie plate and center gelatin on serving plate.

High Spirits

Let your kids help decorate the front porch with ghostly paper wind socks that come alive in the breeze. For each wind sock, draw spooky eyes and a scary mouth on an 18x6-inch piece of white construction paper. Bring the long edges of the construction paper together to form a tube and staple the ends together. Cut eight 8-foot-long strips of white crepe paper. Drape the strips over the tube with both ends hanging down to create "tails"; secure with tape. For a hanger, cut a 30-inch piece of string; staple string ends to opposite sides at the top of the wind sock.

Creepy Crawly Gelatin

Pumpkin Cupcakes

Bake these treats in colorful Halloween paper bake cups.
You'll find the papers in the cake decorating section at a supermarket
or kitchenware store (photo, pages 10–11).

Prep time: 15 minutes
Baking time: 20 minutes plus cooling

1   package (2-layer size) white
    cake mix *or* cake mix with
    pudding in the mix
¼   cup KOOL-AID Orange Flavor
    Sugar-Sweetened Soft Drink
    Mix
1   container (16 ounces) ready-
    to-spread vanilla frosting

Prepare and bake cake mix as directed
on package for cupcakes, adding soft
drink mix before beating.

Frost cooled cupcakes with frosting.

Sprinkle with additional soft drink mix to
resemble pumpkins. Create a "face" with
Halloween candies, decorating gel and
decorating icing.

Makes 24 cupcakes.

Note: To color frosting, stir 1 tablespoon
KOOL-AID Orange Flavor Sugar-
Sweetened Soft Drink Mix into frosting
until well blended.

Caramel Coffee

Brew a pot of this delicious coffee to serve the adults
who tag along with their youngsters on the trick-or-treat route.

Prep time: 10 minutes

6   tablespoons MAXWELL HOUSE
    Coffee, any variety
½   cup KRAFT Caramel Dessert
    Topping
4½ cups cold water

Place coffee in filter in brew basket of coffeemaker. Place topping in empty pot of coffeemaker. Prepare coffee with cold water. When brewing is complete, stir until well mixed. Top each serving with thawed COOL WHIP Whipped Topping and chopped chocolate-covered toffee, if desired.

Makes 6 servings.

Caramel Coffee

SILLY not scary Halloween

If you're planning a party for little ones who may be afraid of witches, devils and ghosts, try these ideas for celebrating the magical qualities of Halloween. Take the fear, not the fun, out of Halloween with these delightfully easy foods and party tips. When you serve snacks with kid-pleasing ingredients and silly names, such as Bologna Wiggles and GHOUL-AID® Punch, any party is bound to have a happy ending.

Creepy JIGGLERS® (recipe, page 34)
and Cheezy Nachos (recipe, page 27)

Mummy Wrap

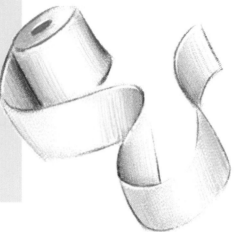

Here is a great game for any Halloween get-together. Divide the guests into teams of two and give each team a roll of toilet tissue. On each team, have one person wrap the other with the tissue. Whichever team gets done wrapping their mummy first, wins. Remember, the entire roll of toilet tissue must be used!

BOOlogna Snackers (recipe, opposite page)

BOOlogna Snackers

Your youngsters can choose the silly shapes they like best for these
fun sandwiches. Ghost-, pumpkin-, moon-, star- and cat-shaped cookie cutters
all work well (photo, opposite page).

White bread slices (optional)
OSCAR MAYER Bologna Slices
KRAFT Singles Pasteurized
Process Cheese Food

Alternate layers of bread, bologna and
process cheese food on cutting board.

Cut into decorative shapes using
Halloween-shaped cookie cutters
or sharp knife.

Decorate with KRAFT Pure Prepared
Mustard, catsup and cut-up process
cheese food.

Cheezy Nachos

Make these nachos extra festive by using blue or other colored tortilla chips
and adding a few sliced olives (photo, pages 24–25).

Prep time: 5 minutes
Microwave time: 2 minutes

1   jar (16 ounces) CHEEZ WHIZ
    Pasteurized Process Cheese
    Sauce
1   package (8 to 11 ounces) tortilla
    chips

Microwave process cheese sauce
as directed on label.

Arrange chips on large serving tray.

Pour process cheese sauce over chips.
Serve immediately.

Makes 4 to 6 servings.

Hot Broccoli Cheese Dip

Set out this bubbling dip with an assortment of fresh veggies and
slices of cocktail bread and let the party begin!

Prep time: 5 minutes
Baking time: 15 minutes

2 cups KRAFT Finely Shredded
   Mild Cheddar Cheese
1 package (10 ounces) frozen
   chopped broccoli, thawed,
   well drained
1 package (8 ounces)
   PHILADELPHIA Cream
   Cheese, softened
1 cup BREAKSTONE'S *or*
   KNUDSEN Sour Cream
1 envelope GOOD SEASONS
   Mild Italian Salad Dressing Mix

Mix all ingredients until well blended.

Spoon into 9-inch pie plate.

Bake at 350°F for 15 minutes or until
cheese is melted. Garnish with green
onions and pearl red onions. Serve with
assorted cut-up fresh vegetables and
cocktail bread slices.

Makes 3½ cups.

Hot Broccoli Cheese Dip

Bologna Wiggles

These tummy ticklers are sure to please hungry Halloween celebrants (photo, page 33).

Prep time: 5 minutes

2 slices OSCAR MAYER Bologna
1 tablespoon MIRACLE WHIP
   Salad Dressing
1 hamburger bun, split

Stack bologna slices on cutting board. Cut into very thin strips.

Place bologna strips in small bowl; stir to separate.

Spread bun with salad dressing. Fill with bologna strips.

Makes 1 sandwich.

Keep It Simple

The costumes for preschoolers don't have to be elaborate. Give your youngsters some simple ideas and let them choose what they want to be. An animal, such as a bunny, mouse or cat, is especially cute. Then, start with a sweatshirt, add a few decorative touches and paint the child's face. Painting kids' faces is a smart alternative to masks. Masks often frighten young children and may block their vision when they're climbing steps or crossing the street.

America's Favorite Grilled Cheese Sandwich

America's Favorite Grilled Cheese Sandwich

Hosting a kids' party? Give them orange balloons to draw
pumpkin faces on. It will keep them busy while you grill the sandwiches,
plus you get some last-minute party decorations.

Prep time: 5 minutes
Cooking time: 5 minutes

2 slices bread
2 KRAFT Singles Pasteurized
   Process Cheese Food
2 teaspoons butter *or* margarine,
   softened

Top 1 bread slice with process cheese
food and second bread slice.

Spread outside of sandwich with butter.

Cook in skillet on medium heat until
lightly browned on both sides.

Makes 1 sandwich.

Grilled Cheese for a Crowd: For each
sandwich, top a bread slice with a slice
of KRAFT Singles Pasteurized Process
Cheese Food and a second bread slice.
Spread the outside of each sandwich
with butter *or* margarine. Place
sandwiches on a cookie sheet. Bake
in a 350°F oven for 5 to 8 minutes on
each side or until golden brown and
cheese is melted.

Take-Home Treats

Your party guests won't want
to wait to get their hands on
these Halloween handouts.
Begin by washing some new large
clear plastic gloves (look for them
at beauty supply stores). Stand the
gloves over long-necked bottles to
dry. Stick one piece of candy corn
at the tip of each finger, pointed
side down, for fingernails. Fill the
glove with Haunted Snack Mix
(recipe, page 35), Trick or Treat
Snack Mix (recipe, page 64),
popcorn or caramel corn.
Tie a bow at the wrist with
ribbon or yarn.

Black & Orange Spook Cups

Any little gremlin, ballerina, fairy princess or clown will
howl with delight at this party treat.

Prep time: 15 minutes plus refrigerating

4	cups cold milk, divided
1	package (4-serving size) JELL-O Chocolate Fudge Flavor Instant Pudding & Pie Filling
10	to 12 (7-ounce) glasses *or* clear plastic cups
1	package (4-serving size) JELL-O Vanilla Instant Pudding & Pie Filling
	Few drops *each* yellow and red food coloring
12	chocolate sandwich cookies, crushed
	Halloween sprinkles

Pour 2 cups of the milk into large bowl. Add chocolate fudge flavor pudding mix. Beat with wire whisk 2 minutes. Fill glasses about ½ full with pudding mixture.

Pour remaining 2 cups milk into another large bowl. Add vanilla flavor pudding mix. Beat with wire whisk 2 minutes. Stir in a few drops food colorings to tint mixture orange. Spoon orange mixture evenly over chocolate mixture. Top with crushed cookies.

Refrigerate until ready to serve. Garnish with Halloween sprinkles.

Makes 10 to 12 servings.

Note: Pudding cups can also be served frozen. Use plastic or paper cups, not glasses. Freeze 3 hours or until firm.

Picking Pumpkins

The secret to spooky or silly jack-o'-lanterns is to choose the right pumpkin. Look for firm ones that stand upright without tipping. Select a pumpkin that fits the design you want to carve or paint. Rounded pumpkins are ideal for jolly faces, while tall, narrow pumpkins make really scary "monsters." For a face with "warts" look for a pumpkin with blotches.

Bologna Wiggles (recipe, page 29) and Black & Orange Spook Cups (recipe, opposite page)

Creepy JIGGLERS®

Another time, instead of using molds, simply double this recipe and pour into a 13x9-inch pan. Refrigerate and then cut into Halloween shapes with cookie cutters (photo, pages 24–25).

Prep time: 10 minutes
Refrigerating time: 3 hours

1¼ cups boiling water (do not add cold water)
1 package (8-serving size) *or* 2 packages (4-serving size *each*) JELL-O Gelatin Dessert, any flavor

Using paper towel dipped in vegetable oil, lightly wipe inside of mold. (Or, spray mold lightly with no stick cooking spray.)

Stir boiling water into gelatin in medium bowl at least 3 minutes until completely dissolved. Pour into mold to within ⅛ inch of top.

Refrigerate at least 3 hours or until firm. (Gelatin does not stick to finger when touched.) Dip bottom of mold in warm water about 15 seconds. Pull gelatin away from all edges of mold with index finger. Slip finger underneath Creepy JIGGLERS and gently lift from mold.

Makes 10.

"Black" JIGGLERS: Use 1 package (4-serving size) *each* JELL-O Orange Flavor and Grape Flavor Gelatin Dessert.

Note: Do not swallow JIGGLERS whole.

Abracadabra!

Youngsters can have fun providing magical entertainment at Halloween gatherings with these mom-approved tricks. The tricks are especially easy because they use items you probably have around the house.

• **Magic Milk:** Place a few drops of food coloring in the bottom of a drinking glass. Pour white milk into the glass and watch the audience's surprise as the milk turns color.

• **Amazing Finger:** Put a little dish soap on your index finger without anyone knowing. Fill a small bowl with water; sprinkle pepper on top. Invite an audience member to test his or her finger for magic by poking it into the bowl. (Nothing happens.) When you poke your finger into the water, the pepper shoots to the edges of the bowl. Abracadabra!

Haunted Snack Mix

Here's an easy-to-make recipe that kids can prepare and package themselves.

Prep time: 5 minutes

4   cups POST Halloween
     WAFFLE CRISP Cereal
1½ cups miniature marshmallows
1   cup BAKER'S Semi-Sweet Real
     Chocolate Chips *or*
     4 chocolate candy bars
     (1.55 ounces *each*), broken
     into rectangles

Mix all ingredients in large bowl.
Serve as a snack.

Makes 6½ cups.

Variation: Prepare as directed,
substituting POST Halloween
HONEYCOMB Sweetened Corn
and Oat Cereal for POST Halloween
WAFFLE CRISP Cereal.

Haunted Snack Mix

GHOUL-AID® Punch

Dress up the ice cubes for this fruity punch by freezing a maraschino cherry or a mandarin orange section in the center of each cube.

Prep time: 10 minutes

1 envelope KOOL-AID Cherry Flavor Unsweetened Soft Drink Mix

1 envelope KOOL-AID Grape Flavor Unsweetened Soft Drink Mix

1 envelope KOOL-AID Tropical Punch Flavor Unsweetened Soft Drink Mix

2¾ cups sugar

18 cups cold water (4½ quarts) Ice cubes

Place soft drink mixes and sugar in large punch bowl. Add water; stir to dissolve. Serve over ice cubes.

Makes 18 servings.

Variation: Prepare as directed except omit sugar and substitute KOOL-AID Sugar-Sweetened Soft Drink Mixes for the Unsweetened KOOL-AID.

Pick-a-Theme Party

f you're hosting a Halloween party for smaller children, make it lighthearted and pleasant. Tone down the terror and go for the fantasy. Here are some party-theme ideas to try:

• **Barnyard Bash:** Suggest your young guests dress up as their favorite barnyard animals.

• **Cool Cats Party:** Ask your guests to come as cats. Suggest cartoon cats or let them come up with their own creations.

• **Circus Party:** Invite the kids to come dressed as clowns or their favorite circus animals.

• **Wild West Party:** Ask the guests to come dressed as cowboys and cowgirls or something else related to the Wild West.

GHOUL-AID® Punch (recipe, opposite page) and
Trick or Treat Snack Mix (recipe, page 64)

party at the PUMPKIN patch

Whether set at a pumpkin patch or in your own backyard, this outdoor party is a winning recipe for Halloween fun. It's easy to get in the festive spirit with this collection of tricks, such as painting pumpkins and making your own piñatas and treats, including Goblin Goo Drink and Witch's Web dessert.

Southwest Ranch Cheeseburgers
(recipe, page 46)

Italian Vegetable Dip

Keep the ingredients for this easy-fixing, boldly flavored dip
on hand for impromptu get-togethers.

Prep time: 10 minutes plus refrigerating

1 cup BREAKSTONE'S *or* KNUDSEN Sour Cream

1 cup KRAFT Mayo Real Mayonnaise

1 envelope GOOD SEASONS Zesty Italian Salad Dressing Mix

¼ cup *each* finely chopped green and red peppers

Mix sour cream, mayo and salad dressing mix.

Stir in green and red peppers. Refrigerate.

Serve with assorted cut-up vegetables, boiled potatoes, breadsticks or chips.

Makes 2¼ cups.

40

Italian Vegetable Dip

Giggle and Grab

Kids love surprises and what better way to package them than in a piñata. You can purchase a Halloween piñata or gather the kids together and make your own. Here's how: Soak strips of newspaper in liquid starch and wrap them in layers around an inflated balloon. Let dry completely. Cut a hole in the top of the hardened shell, pop the balloon and fill the piñata with goodies. Patch the hole and decorate with tissue paper and/or paints.

Hot Bacon Cheese Spread

Your guests will love the way this creamy dip is served in a hollowed-out loaf of bread. You can reheat the dip, bread bowl and all, in your microwave oven.

Prep time: 15 minutes
Baking time: 1 hour

1   loaf (16 ounces) round bread
12 slices OSCAR MAYER Center Cut Bacon, crisply cooked, crumbled
1   package (8 ounces) KRAFT Shredded Colby/Monterey Jack Cheese
1   cup (4 ounces) KRAFT 100% Grated Parmesan Cheese
1   cup KRAFT Mayo Real Mayonnaise
1   small onion, finely chopped
1   clove garlic, minced

Cut lengthwise slice from top of bread loaf, remove center, leaving 1-inch-thick shell. Cut removed bread into bite-size pieces; set aside.

Mix remaining ingredients in small bowl. Spoon into hollowed bread shell. Cover shell with top of bread; place on cookie sheet.

Bake at 350°F for 1 hour. Serve with bread pieces or crackers.

Makes 3½ cups.

Note: *To reheat,* microwave filled bread shell with top on HIGH 1 to 2 minutes or until thoroughly heated, stirring once.

Hot Bacon Cheese Spread

Bologna Pumpkin Head

party at the PUMPKIN patch

Bologna Pumpkin Head

For an outdoor party, don't forget to have an old-fashioned, three-legged race.

For each team, tie two people's legs together with a scarf (or use a gunny sack).

Then, start the race. The winning team gets to eat this sandwich first.

OSCAR MAYER Bologna
Flour tortilla
KRAFT Singles Pasteurized
  Process Cheese Food, cut
  into pieces
KRAFT Pure Prepared Mustard
Catsup

Place bologna slice on tortilla. Create a "face" using process cheese food, mustard and catsup.

TACO BELL® HOME ORIGINALS™ 2-Step Taco Dip

TACO BELL® HOME ORIGINALS™
2-Step Taco Dip

Going next door for a Halloween bash? Take along
this south-of-the-border party snack.

You only need:

1   container (16 ounces)
      BREAKSTONE'S *or* KNUDSEN
      Sour Cream
1   package (1¼ ounces)
      TACO BELL HOME ORIGINALS
      Taco Seasoning Mix
1   cup *each* shredded lettuce and
      chopped tomato
1   cup KRAFT Mexican Style
      Shredded Cheese

1. PREP IT QUICK! Mix sour cream
and seasoning mix until well blended.
Spread on bottom of 9-inch pie plate
or quiche dish.

2. PILE ON THE FUN!™ Layer
remaining ingredients over sour cream
mixture. Garnish with green pepper
cut-outs, sliced pitted ripe olives, small
halved tomato slice and fresh chives
to create a "cat's face." Serve with
tortilla chips.

Makes 6 to 8 servings.

TACO BELL and HOME ORIGINALS are trademarks owned
and licensed by Taco Bell Corp.

Pumkin Fun

Play up pumpkins at your outdoor party with this version of ring toss.
Paint point values (10, 20, 30, etc.) on pumpkins and arrange them
with the highest value farthest from the starting line. Have players
stand, one at a time, on the line and try to toss a large plastic hoop around
a pumpkin. Give each participant three tries; the highest score wins!

Southwest Ranch Cheeseburgers

Serve these thick, juicy burgers with chips, pickles and fresh fruit
for an easy supper anytime (photo, pages 38–39).

Prep time: 10 minutes
Cooking time: 12 minutes

1   **pound ground beef**
8   **KRAFT Deluxe Pasteurized Process American Cheese Slices**
4   **Kaiser rolls, split, toasted**
¼   **cup KRAFT Ranch Dressing**
8   **slices OSCAR MAYER Bacon, crisply cooked**
    TACO BELL HOME ORIGINALS Thick 'N Chunky Salsa

Shape meat into 4 patties.

Cook patties in skillet on medium heat 4 to 6 minutes on each side or to desired doneness.

Top each patty with 2 process cheese slices; cover. Continue cooking until process cheese is melted. Fill rolls with cheeseburgers; top with dressing and bacon. Serve with salsa.

Makes 4 sandwiches.

Grilling directions: Grill patties over hot coals 8 to 12 minutes or to desired doneness. Continue as directed.

TACO BELL and HOME ORIGINALS are trademarks owned and licensed by Taco Bell Corp.

Halloween Grillout

When your Halloween plans call for an outdoor gathering, there's no easier or tastier way to feed everyone than with burgers cooked outside—on the grill. With recipes such as Southwest Ranch Cheeseburgers (recipe, above) or BBQ Bacon Cheeseburgers (recipe, page 47), you can grill a delicious meal for all your hungry ghosts and goblins and still get in on every minute of the party.

BBQ Bacon Cheeseburgers

party at the PUMPKIN patch

BBQ Bacon Cheeseburgers

Toasting the rolls makes these great sandwiches even better. Place the roll halves, cut sides down, on the grill rack. Grill about 1 minute or until lightly toasted.

Prep time: 15 minutes
Grilling time: 12 minutes

1 pound ground beef
2 tablespoons KRAFT Original Barbecue Sauce
8 KRAFT Deluxe Pasteurized Process American Cheese Slices
4 Kaiser rolls *or* hamburger rolls, split, toasted
Lettuce
4 slices OSCAR MAYER Bacon, crisply cooked
Tomato slices (optional)

Mix meat and barbecue sauce. Shape into 4 patties.

Place patties on grill over hot coals. Grill 8 to 12 minutes or to desired doneness, brushing occasionally with additional barbecue sauce.

Top each patty with 2 process cheese slices. Continue grilling until process cheese is melted. Fill rolls with lettuce, cheeseburgers, bacon and tomato.

Makes 4 sandwiches.

47

Halloween Coffee Cupcakes

Let the little helpers at your house frost these sweet treats.

Prep time: 10 minutes
Baking time: 25 minutes plus cooling

1 package (2-layer size) chocolate cake mix
 Chilled freshly brewed double-strength MAXWELL HOUSE Coffee, any variety
 Coffee Pudding Frosting (recipe, below)

Prepare cake mix as directed on package, substituting coffee for water.

Spoon into paper-lined muffin pan, filling each cup ½ full.

Bake as directed on package for cupcakes. Cool. Frost with Coffee Pudding Frosting. Refrigerate until ready to serve. Decorate with chocolate sprinkles and candy coffee beans, if desired.

Makes 24 cupcakes.

Coffee Pudding Frosting

The subtle coffee flavor of this luscious frosting complements the
Halloween Coffee Cupcakes (recipe, above) or any chocolate or yellow cake.
Be sure to store the frosted cake in the refrigerator.

Prep time: 10 minutes

½ cup chilled freshly brewed double-strength MAXWELL HOUSE Coffee, any variety
½ cup cold milk
1 package (4-serving size) JELL-O Vanilla *or* Chocolate Flavor Instant Pudding & Pie Filling
1 tub (8 ounces) COOL WHIP Whipped Topping, thawed

Pour coffee and milk into medium bowl. Add pudding mix. Beat with wire whisk 1 minute. Immediately stir in whipped topping. Spread on cupcakes.

Makes about 4 cups.

Halloween Coffee Cupcakes

Witch's Web

Dress this creamy dessert in Halloween style by using decorating icing
to create a spiderweb. Make the spider by inserting licorice "legs" into a
huge gumdrop and adding tiny red candies for eyes.

Prep time: 15 minutes
Refrigerating time: 1 hour

2 packages (12.6 ounces *each*)
JELL-O No Bake Cookies &
Creme Dessert
⅔ cup butter *or* margarine, melted
2⅔ cups cold milk

Stir Crust Mix and butter thoroughly with spoon in 13x9-inch pan until crumbs are well moistened. Press firmly onto bottom of pan.

Pour cold milk into deep, narrow-bottom bowl. Add Filling Mix. Beat with electric mixer on low speed 30 seconds. Beat on high speed 3 minutes. **Do not underbeat.** Stir Crushed Cookies into filling until well blended. Spread filling mixture over crust. Garnish with decorating icing and candies to create "spiderweb" and "spider."

Refrigerate at least 1 hour until set. To serve, dip bottom of pan in hot water for 30 seconds for easier cutting and serving. Store leftover dessert, covered, in refrigerator.

Makes 15 servings.

Paint a Pumpkin

Not every pumpkin is meant to be carved. So why not let your kids paint their pumpkins instead? This way, children won't need to use knives for carving, the uncut pumpkins will last longer and the youngsters can paint on as many small details as they like. For extra fun, add tufts of yarn or other trims to dress up the jack-o'-lanterns.

Here's how to go about it: Working outside, cover a picnic table with a disposable tablecloth or newspapers. Set out acrylic paints, paintbrushes and plastic containers filled with water for rinsing the brushes. Draw an outline of a face on each pumpkin and let the kids fill in with the paint. Or, turn the kids loose with shaped sponges or markers and watch the fun they have creating silly, surprised or scary faces.

Spooky Ghost Cups

Spooky Ghost Cups

Need a kid-friendly centerpiece for an outdoor party? Start with a
pumpkin and about 2 pounds of large gumdrops. Stick one end of a toothpick
into each gumdrop and poke the toothpicks into the pumpkin.
Your pumpkin will look like one giant gumdrop.

Prep time: 15 minutes plus refrigerating

2 cups cold milk
2 packages (4-serving size *each*)
    JELL-O Vanilla Flavor Instant
    Pudding & Pie Filling
2 cups thawed COOL WHIP
    Whipped Topping
8 (7-ounce) clear plastic cups
    or glasses

Pour cold milk into large bowl. Add
pudding mixes. Beat with wire whisk
2 minutes. Gently stir in whipped
topping.

Spoon mixture into large zipper-style
plastic bag. Close bag tightly. Snip
½-inch piece off one corner of bag.
Holding top of bag tightly, squeeze
mixture into small plastic cups to
resemble ghosts. Create a "face"
with decorating icing and candies.

Refrigerate until ready to serve.

Makes 8 servings.

PHILADELPHIA 3-STEP® Double Layer Pumpkin Cheesecake

Make gumdrop cut-outs for a colorful garnish on this luscious cheesecake. To do so, roll out a large gumdrop on a sugared surface. Then, cut out fancy shapes using small cookie cutters.

Prep time: 10 minutes
Baking time: 40 minutes plus cooling
Refrigerating time: 3 hours

2 packages (8 ounces *each*) PHILADELPHIA Cream Cheese, softened
½ cup sugar
½ teaspoon vanilla
2 eggs
½ cup canned pumpkin
½ teaspoon ground cinnamon Dash *each* ground cloves and nutmeg
1 ready-to-use graham cracker crumb crust (6 ounces *or* 9 inches)

1. **Mix** cream cheese, sugar and vanilla with electric mixer on medium speed until well blended. Add eggs; mix until blended. Remove 1 cup batter; stir in pumpkin and spices.

2. **Pour** remaining plain batter into crust. Top with pumpkin batter.

3. **Bake** at 350°F for 40 minutes or until center is almost set. Cool. Refrigerate 3 hours or overnight. Garnish with thawed COOL WHIP Whipped Topping and gumdrop cut-outs.

Makes 8 servings.

**PHILADELPHIA 3-STEP® Double Layer
Pumpkin Cheesecake**

Spidery Webs

K ids will love this wicked marble-art spiderweb project. Cut circles from black construction paper so they just fit inside disposable cake pans or pie plates. Carefully roll marbles in small cups of white tempera paint. With plastic spoons, remove the marbles and drop them into the cake pans or pie plates. Have the kids rock the pans from side to side (for a more intricate web, dip the marbles a second time). While the paint is still wet, sprinkle glow-in-the-dark glitter on the webs. Once the webs are dry, head for a dark room to see the creations glow.

Two Color Goo and Goblin Goo Drink
(recipes, opposite page)

Goblin Goo Drink

Boil, bubble, toil and trouble! Create your own witch's cauldron by serving this kid-pleasing punch from a deep, black pot or kettle.

Prep time: 15 minutes
Refrigerating time: 4 hours

1 package (8-serving size) *or*
   2 packages (4-serving size *each*) JELL-O Grape *or* Orange Flavor Gelatin Dessert
4 cups (1 quart) cold prepared KOOL-AID Grape *or* Orange Flavor Soft Drink Mix

Prepare gelatin as directed on package.

Refrigerate 4 hours or until firm.

Break gelatin into small flakes with fork. Spoon about ½ cup gelatin into each of 8 tall glasses. Pour ½ cup cold soft drink over gelatin in each glass. Serve immediately with a straw to sip gelatin pieces and soft drink.

Makes 8 servings.

Two Color Goo: Prepare grape and orange flavor gelatin as directed on package. Refrigerate and break into flakes as directed. Layer ¼ cup orange (or grape) gelatin flakes, ¼ cup grape (or orange) gelatin flakes and additional ¼ cup orange (or grape) gelatin flakes in each glass. Pour cold orange soft drink over gelatin in each glass.

Fizzy Goblin Goo: Just before serving, prepare KOOL-AID as directed, substituting cold seltzer for water.

Fresh Air Halloween

Break with tradition and celebrate this Halloween outdoors. Create a buffet by arranging bales of straw into a table or using a picnic table. Then, set out lots of nibble or finger foods so your hungry guests can stop by between activities to sample the treats.

no tricks
just TREATS

Here's a first-rate assortment of goodies and confections just right for toting to a school party or handing out when the little gremlins come calling on trick-or-treat night. Ghouls and bats of all ages will be happily spooked by Halloween treats such as Candy Corn Popcorn Balls and JELL-O® Ween Poke Brownies.

JELL-O® Ween Poke Brownies (recipe, page 65)

OREO O's™ Bars

These chewy, gooey treats are so easy to make you'll want to fix a batch
to tote to a party and prepare another batch to treat the family.

Prep time: 5 minutes plus cooling
Microwave time: 3 minutes

¼ cup (½ stick) butter *or*
   margarine
1 package (10½ ounces) miniature
   marshmallows (6 cups)
8 cups POST OREO O's Cereal

Microwave butter in 4-quart
microwavable bowl on HIGH 45 seconds
or until melted. Add marshmallows; mix
to coat. Microwave 1½ minutes or until
marshmallows are melted and smooth,
stirring after 45 seconds. Add cereal;
mix to coat well.

Press firmly into greased foil-lined
13x9-inch pan. Cool; cut into rectangles.

Makes 18.

Chocolate OREO O's™ Bars: Prepare
as directed, melting 2 squares BAKER'S
Semi-Sweet Baking Chocolate with
butter.

OREO O's is a trademark of Nabisco Brands Co. Used
under license.

Keep It Fun!

Kids love scaring the daylights out of adults on Halloween.
Follow these safety tips to help your trick-or-treaters avoid giving
you some real scares:

• Outfit each trick-or-treater with a flashlight.
• Tell your kids not to walk or run across yards. Lawn ornaments,
  shrubs and clotheslines can be difficult to see in the dark.
• Review traffic safety rules with your children.
• Go trick-or-treating in a group. An adult should accompany
  small children and set a time for older children
  to return home.

OREO O's™ Bars

Candy Corn Popcorn Balls

Candy Corn Popcorn Balls

Use this yummy treat for prizes in a pumpkin race. Divide kids into two groups. Give each group a pumpkin and have them race to the finish line while rolling the pumpkin with their hands.

Prep time: 15 minutes
Microwave time: 2 minutes

¼ cup (½ stick) butter *or* margarine
1 package (10½ ounces) miniature marshmallows (6 cups)
1 package (4-serving size) JELL-O Gelatin Dessert, any flavor
12 cups (3 quarts) popped popcorn
1 cup candy corn

Microwave butter and marshmallows in large microwavable bowl on HIGH 1½ to 2 minutes or until marshmallows are puffed. Stir in gelatin until well mixed.

Pour marshmallow mixture over popcorn and candy corn in large bowl. Mix lightly until well coated. Shape into 15 balls or other shapes with greased or wet hands. Wrap each ball in plastic wrap and tie with raffia or ribbon, if desired.

Makes 15.

A Little at a Time

Kids love to dig in and devour their Halloween treats. To keep them happy, yet avoid upset stomachs, have them select a few treats to enjoy as soon as they return from trick-or-treating. Then, set the remaining treats aside and let them choose a few each day.

63

Trick or Treat Snack Mix

Keep the kids entertained on a rainy October afternoon by having them decorate small bags to package this terrific treat (photo, page 37). You provide the paper bags, markers and Halloween stickers and let the youngsters do the rest.

Prep time: 5 minutes

4 cups POST Halloween
    HONEYCOMB Sweetened
    Corn and Oat Cereal
2 cups caramel popcorn
2 cups small pretzels
1 cup candy corn

Mix all ingredients in large bowl. Serve as a snack.

Makes about 9 cups.

Snack Treats

For a spur-of-the-moment Halloween get-together, JELL-O Pudding Chocolate & Orange Swirl Snacks and JELL-O Gelatin Orange & Scary Berry Black Gelatin Snacks provide you with a dessert or snack that is easy and colorful. (You may even want to add a dollop of thawed COOL WHIP Whipped Topping to your pudding snacks.) To keep the snacks chilled, arrange them in a large bowl filled with ice. Or, hollow out a pumpkin, line with foil or plastic wrap, add a layer of ice and pile high with the snacks.

Snack Treats: JELL-O® Pudding and Gelatin Snacks

JELL-O® Ween Poke Brownies

Two treats in one! Pudding and brownies share center stage in this very special Halloween dessert (photo, below and pages 58–59).

Prep time: 30 minutes plus refrigerating
Baking time: 35 minutes

  1 package (19.8 ounces) brownie
     mix
1½ cups cold milk
  1 package (4-serving size) JELL-O
     Vanilla Flavor Instant Pudding
     & Pie Filling
     Few drops *each* red and yellow
     food coloring

JELL-O® Ween Poke Brownies

Prepare and bake brownie mix as directed on package for 8- or 9-inch square baking pan. Remove from oven. Immediately use round handle of wooden spoon to poke holes at 1-inch intervals down through brownies to pan.

Pour cold milk into large bowl. Add pudding mix. Beat with wire whisk 2 minutes. Stir in a few drops food colorings to tint mixture orange. Quickly pour about ½ of the thin pudding evenly over warm brownies and into holes. Tap pan lightly to fill holes. Let remaining pudding mixture stand to thicken slightly. Spread remaining pudding over top of brownies to "frost."

Refrigerate 1 hour or until ready to serve. Cut into 2-inch squares. Cut each square diagonally into triangles.

Makes 32.

Coconut Macaroons

Dip these coconut puffs into chocolate for an exceptional treat.

Prep time: 10 minutes
Baking time per cookie sheet: 20 minutes
  plus cooling

2⅔ cups (7 ounces)
    BAKER'S ANGEL FLAKE
    Coconut
⅔ cup sugar
6 tablespoons flour
¼ teaspoon salt
4 egg whites
1 teaspoon almond extract
    Whole natural almonds
    (optional)

Mix coconut, sugar, flour and salt in large bowl. Stir in egg whites and almond extract until well blended.

Drop by teaspoonfuls onto greased and floured cookie sheets. Press 1 almond into center of each cookie.

Bake at 325°F for 20 minutes or until edges of cookies are golden brown. Immediately remove from cookie sheets. Cool on wire racks.

Makes about 3 dozen.

Chocolate-Dipped Macaroons:
Prepare macaroons as directed; cool. Melt 1 package (8 squares) BAKER'S Semi-Sweet Baking Chocolate as directed on package. Dip cookies halfway into chocolate; let excess chocolate drip off. Let stand at room temperature or refrigerate on wax paper-lined tray 30 minutes or until chocolate is firm.

Coconut Macaroons and
Chocolate-Dipped Macaroons

Costume Safety

In many communities, trick-or-treating is a favorite tradition. Here are
some hints to help assure that your child makes the rounds safely
and happily:

• Instead of a mask, which can slip down and limit a child's vision,
  use face paint or makeup.

• Choose light and bright colors for costumes. Add glow-in-the-dark
  or reflective tape.

• Make sure the costume fits well. Check that the sleeves and pant
  legs aren't so long that the child might get tangled up or trip.

• Dress children in their own shoes. Wearing high heels or shoes that
  are too big can be dangerous and uncomfortable.

Cookies & Creme Scream

Suit your fancy—tint this rich dessert pastel, bright or any shade of orange inbetween just by varying the amount of food colorings you add.

Prep time: 15 minutes
Freezing time: 2 hours

1   **package (12.6 ounces) JELL-O No Bake Cookies & Creme Dessert**
⅓   **cup butter *or* margarine, melted**
1⅓   **cups cold milk**
    Few drops *each* red and yellow food coloring

Stir Crust Mix and butter thoroughly with fork in medium bowl until crumbs are well moistened. Press mixture onto bottoms of 12 to 15 paper-lined muffin cups.

Pour cold milk into deep, narrow-bottom bowl. Add Filling Mix. Beat with electric mixer on low speed 30 seconds. Stir in a few drops food colorings to tint mixture orange; beat on high speed 3 minutes. **Do not underbeat.**

Reserve ½ cup Crushed Cookies. Gently stir remaining Crushed Cookies into filling until well blended. Divide prepared filling mix among cups. Top with reserved ½ cup Crushed Cookies.

Freeze 2 hours or until firm. Remove from freezer. Garnish with assorted decorative candies. Store leftover dessert, covered, in freezer up to 2 weeks.

Makes 12 to 15 servings.

Cheesy Popcorn

Fill a bowl with your favorite popcorn and make it special by sprinkling on KRAFT Macaroni & Cheese Cheese Topping. There will be Halloween magic as you watch it disappear!

Cookies & Creme Scream
and Cheesy Popcorn

Double Banana Streusel Cake

Double Banana Streusel Cake

Layers of moist banana cake and crunchy banana streusel
topping make this cake doubly delicious. Serve it with hot cider
as a treat for a Halloween gathering at your house.

Prep time: 15 minutes
Baking time: 55 minutes plus cooling

1 cup POST
   MORNING TRADITIONS
   BANANA NUT CRUNCH Cereal
½ cup firmly packed brown sugar
1 teaspoon ground cinnamon
1 package (2-layer size) banana
   cake mix
4 eggs
1 cup BREAKSTONE'S *or*
   KNUDSEN Sour Cream
½ cup oil
   Powdered Sugar Glaze
   (recipe follows)

Mix cereal, sugar and cinnamon in small
bowl. Beat cake mix, eggs, sour cream
and oil in large bowl with electric mixer
on low speed just to moisten, scraping
side of bowl often. Beat on medium
speed 4 minutes.

Pour ⅓ of the batter into greased and
floured 12-cup fluted tube pan or
10-inch tube pan. Sprinkle with ⅓ of
the cereal mixture. Repeat layers twice,
ending with cereal mixture.

Bake at 350°F for 50 to 55 minutes or
until cake tester inserted in center comes
out clean. Cool 15 minutes in pan on
wire rack; remove from pan. Cool
completely on wire rack. Drizzle with
Powdered Sugar Glaze. Garnish with
additional cereal and walnut halves.

Makes 16 servings.

Powdered Sugar Glaze: Mix
1 cup sifted powdered sugar and
1 tablespoon milk in small bowl. Mix
in additional milk, 1 teaspoon at a
time, until glaze is smooth and of
drizzling consistency.

Lemon Blueberry Morning Cake:
Prepare cake as directed, substituting
1 cup POST MORNING TRADITIONS
BLUEBERRY MORNING Cereal and
1 package (2-layer size) lemon cake mix
for POST MORNING TRADITIONS
BANANA NUT CRUNCH Cereal and
banana cake mix.

Chocolate Chunk Streusel Coffeecake

Get Halloween off to a festive start by serving these moist squares—topped with a nutty, chocolatey crumb topping—with mugs of coffee or glasses of milk.

Prep time: 15 minutes
Baking time: 25 minutes plus cooling

⅔ cup flour
½ cup firmly packed brown sugar
¼ cup (½ stick) butter *or* margarine
⅓ cup chopped slivered almonds
1 package (2-layer size) yellow cake mix
   Cooled freshly brewed double-strength MAXWELL HOUSE Coffee, any variety
6 squares BAKER'S Semi-Sweet Baking Chocolate, chopped

Mix flour and sugar in medium bowl. Cut in butter until mixture resembles coarse crumbs. Stir in almonds.

Prepare cake mix as directed on package, substituting brewed coffee for water. Pour batter into greased 15x10x1-inch baking pan. Sprinkle with chocolate and streusel mixture.

Bake at 350°F for 20 to 25 minutes or until toothpick inserted in center comes out clean. Cool. Cut into squares.

Makes 24 servings.

Jokes and Riddles

All good little ghosts and goblins need a supply of jokes and riddles to share. Have you heard these?

Q. Knock, knock. **A.** Who's there? **Q.** Boo! **A.** Boo who? **A.** Don't cry!

Q. What did the ghost receive when he won first place at the fair?
A. A boo ribbon.

Q. How do baby ghosts keep their feet warm? **A.** They wear BOOtees.

Q. How do ghosts get to the second floor?
A. They take the scares.

Chocolate Chunk Streusel Coffeecake

SPEEDY SUPPERS

With the arrival of fall, cooks say goodbye to the lazy days of summer and hello to busy nights and the "What's for dinner?" dilemma. So, when the kids are anxiously waiting to go trick-or-treating, to soccer practice or elsewhere, turn to these tasty, easy-to-prepare dishes. They'll be enjoyed by the entire family.

TOMBSTONE® Pepperoni Pizza (tip, page 82)

VELVEETA® Cheeseburger Mac

The flavors of two all-time favorites—cheeseburgers and macaroni & cheese—come together in this one quick fixin' combo.

Prep time: 10 minutes
Cooking time: 15 minutes

1	pound ground beef
2¾	cups water
⅓	cup catsup
1	to 2 teaspoons onion powder
2	cups elbow macaroni, uncooked
¾	pound (12 ounces) VELVEETA Prepared Cheese Product, cut up

Brown meat in large skillet; drain.

Stir in water, catsup and onion powder. Bring to boil. Stir in macaroni. Reduce heat to medium-low; cover. Simmer 8 to 10 minutes or until macaroni is tender.

Add prepared cheese product; stir until melted.

Makes 4 to 6 servings.

VELVEETA® Cheeseburger Mac

A Day of Halloween Meals

Make Halloween a day of celebration by beginning the day with a festive breakfast and finishing the day with one of the delectable suppers in this chapter. For breakfast, rename glasses of chocolate milk Black Cats, or mix up orange juice with lemon-lime carbonated beverage and call it a Pumpkin Spritzer. Bake Double Banana Streusel Cake (recipe, page 71) or Chocolate Chunk Streusel Coffeecake (recipe, page 72). Or, buy some chocolate cake doughnuts, frost them and top with Halloween sprinkles. To make Ghost Toast, use a sharp knife to trim toasted bread slices into ghost shapes. Spread cream cheese over each slice and add raisins for eyes and mouth.

Quick Taco Quesadillas

Quick Taco Quesadillas

Dress up this or any other TACO BELL HOME ORIGINALS Dinner Kit
by adding sliced avocado and cheese to the filling.

Prep time: 10 minutes
Baking time: 10 minutes

1 **pound ground beef**
1 **package (16.33 ounces)**
  TACO BELL HOME ORIGINALS
  Soft Taco Dinner Kit
2 **avocados, peeled, sliced**
  (optional)
1 **package (8 ounces) KRAFT**
  Finely Shredded Cheddar
  Cheese

Brown meat; drain. Add Seasoning Mix; prepare as directed on package.

Soften Tortillas as directed on package. Spoon meat mixture over bottom halves of tortillas. Top with avocados and cheese. Drizzle with Taco Sauce. Fold

tortillas in half; place on cookie sheet which has been sprayed with no stick cooking spray.

Bake at 425°F for 8 to 10 minutes. Serve warm with hot sauce, if desired.

Makes 5 main-dish servings or cut each tortilla into thirds for 30 appetizer servings.

Make-ahead tip: Prepare as directed except do not bake; cover. Refrigerate up to 6 hours. When ready to serve, bake, uncovered, at 425°F for 15 to 20 minutes or until thoroughly heated.

TACO BELL and HOME ORIGINALS are trademarks owned and licensed by Taco Bell Corp.

Seasonal Centerpiece

Your kids will love creating a ghostly Halloween centerpiece that's both easy to make and easy on the budget. Begin by selecting two or three butternut squash of different heights. Paint them with white tempera paint, let dry and add mouths and eyes to them with a permanent black marker.

Cheesy Chicken Fajitas

Cheesy Chicken Fajitas

To warm the tortillas in a microwave for these family-pleasing fajitas, wrap them loosely in waxed paper, then microwave on HIGH for 30 to 40 seconds.

Prep time: 20 minutes
Cooking time: 10 minutes

½ pound boneless skinless chicken breasts, cut into thin strips
1 clove garlic, minced
1 medium green *or* red pepper, cut into strips
½ cup sliced red onion
1½ cups KRAFT Finely Shredded Colby & Monterey Jack Cheese
6 flour tortillas (6-inch), warmed
   TACO BELL HOME ORIGINALS Thick 'N Chunky Salsa

Spray skillet with no stick cooking spray. Add chicken and garlic; cook and stir on medium-high heat 5 minutes.

Add green pepper and onion; cook and stir 4 to 5 minutes or until chicken is cooked through and vegetables are tender-crisp.

Place ¼ cup chicken mixture and ¼ cup cheese on center of each tortilla; fold in half. Serve with salsa.

Makes 6 servings.

TACO BELL and HOME ORIGINALS are trademarks owned and licensed by Taco Bell Corp.

Country Ham Sandwiches

Supper is easy when you start with a hearty sandwich and add one or two simple side dishes such as chips, salads, fruits, vegetable relishes or pickles.

Prep time: 10 minutes

½ cup MIRACLE WHIP Salad Dressing *or* KRAFT Mayo Real Mayonnaise

½ teaspoon garlic powder

½ teaspoon pepper

8 slices whole wheat bread Lettuce and tomato slices (optional)

1 package (6 ounces) OSCAR MAYER Smoked Cooked Ham

8 KRAFT Singles Pasteurized Process Cheese Food

Mix salad dressing and seasonings in small bowl.

Spread on bread slices.

Layer 4 of the bread slices each with lettuce, tomato, ham and 2 process cheese food slices. Top with second bread slices.

Makes 4 sandwiches.

Country Ham 'N Apple Sandwiches: Prepare sandwiches as directed, omitting garlic powder and pepper and substituting apple slices for tomato slices.

Country Ham Sandwiches

Grilled Ham & Cheese

Bring on the TOMBSTONE®

For a quick-to-fix supper before a night of trick-or-treating, delight your kids with a TOMBSTONE® Pizza, the Official Pizza of Halloween. Make it delectably fun by topping it with pepper cut-outs of bats and/or half-moons (photo, pages 74–75).

Grilled Ham & Cheese

On those nights when eating in shifts is a must, have these ingredients on hand
so you can grill one sandwich at a time when needed.

Prep time: 5 minutes
Cooking time: 10 minutes

2   slices bread
2   KRAFT Singles Pasteurized
     Process Cheese Food
3   slices OSCAR MAYER Smoked
     Cooked Ham
     Butter *or* margarine, softened

Top 1 bread slice with 1 process cheese
food slice, ham, second process cheese
food slice and second bread slice.

Spread outside of sandwich with butter.

Cook in skillet on medium heat until
lightly browned on both sides.

Makes 1 sandwich.

Grilled Ham, Cheese & Tomato:
Prepare as directed, adding Dijon
mustard and tomato slices to sandwich
before cooking.

Variation: Prepare as directed,
substituting KRAFT 2% Reduced Fat
Milk Singles for KRAFT Singles.

Veggie Pizza

Veggie Pizza

Top this deliciously easy pizza with an assortment of raw veggies
such as sliced carrots, sliced zucchini or yellow summer squash, tiny broccoli
flowerets, asparagus tips, chopped pepper and/or red onion rings.

Prep time: 10 minutes plus refrigerating
Baking time: 13 minutes plus cooling

2 cans (8 ounces *each*) refrigerated crescent dinner rolls
1 tub (6 ounces) CRACKER BARREL Whipped Extra Sharp Cheese
½ cup BREAKSTONE'S *or* KNUDSEN Sour Cream
1½ teaspoons dill weed
1 teaspoon onion salt
5 cups assorted cut-up fresh vegetables

Unroll dough; press onto bottom of foil-lined 15x10x1-inch baking pan.

Bake at 375°F for 11 to 13 minutes or until golden brown; cool.

Mix cheese, sour cream, dill and onion salt until well blended. Spread on crust. Top with vegetables and additional dill. Refrigerate. Cut into small triangles or squares.

Makes 6 servings.

Legend of the Jack-O'-Lantern

According to Irish folklore, one Halloween night Jack tricked the devil into promising not to take his soul. When Jack died, the devil kept his promise and refused Jack entrance to the underworld. But Jack wasn't allowed in heaven either. With nowhere to go, Jack was left to wander the earth with a hollowed-out turnip and a burning coal to light his way. Irish children brought the fable and their Halloween lanterns to America, but pumpkins, being in much greater supply, replaced the turnips.

Meat and Potatoes Salad

Meat and Potatoes Salad

Get a jump on tomorrow's supper. Tonight, put the steak
in the refrigerator to marinate.

Prep time: 10 minutes plus marinating
Grilling time: 15 minutes

1½	cups SEVEN SEAS VIVA Italian Dressing, divided
1	pound beef sirloin steak
½	pound new potatoes, cut into quarters
1	package (10 ounces) mixed salad greens
1	cup tomato wedges
½	cup thinly sliced red onion

Pour 1 cup of the dressing over steak; cover. Refrigerate 4 hours or overnight to marinate. Drain; discard dressing.

Place potatoes in double layer of heavy-duty aluminum foil to form pouch; top with remaining ½ cup dressing.

Grill steak and potato pouch over medium coals 15 minutes or to desired doneness. Cut steak across grain into thin strips. Toss greens, tomato, onion, steak strips and potatoes. Toss with additional dressing, if desired.

Makes 4 servings.

Chicken 'N Peppers Pasta Skillet

Minimize last-minute preparation by cooking the pasta ahead, rinsing it in cold water and refrigerating it until ready to prepare this flavorful recipe.

Prep time: 10 minutes
Cooking time: 10 minutes plus standing

1 pound boneless skinless chicken breasts, chopped

1 green pepper, cut into thin strips

1 jar (14 ounces) spaghetti sauce (about 1½ cups)

2 cups (4 ounces) rotini pasta, cooked, drained

2 cups KRAFT Classic Garlic Italian Style Shredded Cheese, divided

Spray large skillet with no stick cooking spray. Add chicken; cook and stir 5 minutes. Add green pepper; cook and stir until chicken is cooked through and green pepper is tender.

Stir in sauce, rotini and 1 cup of the cheese. Sprinkle with remaining 1 cup cheese; cover. Let stand 1 to 2 minutes or until cheese is melted.

Makes 6 servings.

Chicken 'N Peppers Pasta Skillet

87

15 Minute Chicken & Rice Dinner

SPEEDY SUPPERS

15 Minute Chicken & Rice Dinner

It's true—you can have supper on the table in just 15 minutes
with this super-simple one-dish meal.

Prep/Cooking time: 15 minutes

1   tablespoon oil*
4   small boneless skinless
    chicken breast halves
    (about 1 pound)
1½ cups water *or* milk
1   can (10¾ ounces) condensed
    cream of chicken soup
2   cups MINUTE White Rice,
    uncooked

Heat oil in large nonstick skillet on
medium-high heat. Add chicken; cover.
Cook 4 minutes on each side or until
cooked through. Remove chicken
from skillet.

Add water and soup to skillet; stir.
Bring to boil.

Stir in rice. Top with chicken; cover.
Cook on low heat 5 minutes. Garnish
with fresh oregano.

Makes 4 servings.

Note: Increase oil to 2 tablespoons
if using regular skillet.

88

Time-Saving Products

For those evenings when mealtime is tight, why not take advantage of some of the high-quality convenience products on your supermarket shelves? You'll find:

- Sliced fresh mushrooms
- Packaged torn mixed salad greens
- OSCAR MAYER Meats
- LOUIS RICH CARVING BOARD Turkey or Ham
- Sliced chicken, pork and beef for stir-frying
- KRAFT Macaroni & Cheese Dinners
- TACO BELL HOME ORIGINALS Dinner Kits
- Canned tomato products with added seasonings
- MINUTE Rice
- SHAKE 'N BAKE Seasoned Coating Mixes
- KRAFT Shredded Cheeses
- DI GIORNO Pastas and Sauces
- TOMBSTONE Pizzas
- Frozen mashed potatoes
- JELL-O Instant Pudding & Pie Fillings

TACO BELL and HOME ORIGINALS are trademarks owned and licensed by Taco Bell Corp.

Easy Cheesy Taco Melts

Easy Cheesy Taco Melts

Using the TACO BELL HOME ORIGINALS Soft Taco Dinner Kit, prepare meat as directed. Place 1 KRAFT Singles Pasteurized Process Cheese Food slice on Tortilla. Top with meat and Taco Sauce. Roll up. Microwave on HIGH 15 to 30 seconds or until process cheese food is melted. Top with shredded lettuce, sliced pitted ripe olives, chopped tomato, KRAFT Shredded Cheese, BREAKSTONE'S *or* KNUDSEN Sour Cream and TACO BELL HOME ORIGINALS Thick 'N Chunky Salsa, if desired.

TACO BELL and HOME ORIGINALS are trademarks owned and licensed by Taco Bell Corp.

Cheesy Chili Fries

For chili fries supreme, garnish them with sour cream, chopped avocado and sliced jalapeño peppers.

Prep time: 20 minutes
Microwave time: 2 minutes

1 **package (32 ounces) frozen French fried potatoes**
1 **can (15 ounces) chili, heated as directed on label**
1 **jar (16 ounces) CHEEZ WHIZ Pasteurized Process Cheese Sauce**

Prepare potatoes as directed on package.

Arrange potatoes on large serving platter. Pour hot chili over potatoes.

Microwave process cheese sauce as directed on label. Pour process cheese sauce over chili.

Makes 6 to 8 servings.

Cheesy Chili Fries

INDEX

INDEX CONTINUED...

Metric Cooking Hints

By making a few conversions, cooks in Australia, Canada, and the United Kingdom can use these recipes with confidence. The charts on this page provide a guide for converting measurements from the U.S. customary system, which is used throughout this book, to the imperial and metric systems. There also is a conversion table for oven temperatures to accommodate the differences in oven calibrations.

Product Differences: Most of the ingredients called for in the recipes in this book are available in English-speaking countries. However, some are known by different names. Here are some common American ingredients and their possible counterparts:
■ Sugar is granulated or castor sugar.
■ Powdered sugar is icing sugar.
■ All-purpose flour is plain household flour or white flour. When self-rising flour is used in place of all-purpose flour in a recipe that calls for leavening, omit the leavening agent (baking soda or baking powder) and salt.
■ Light-colored corn syrup is golden syrup.
■ Cornstarch is cornflour.
■ Baking soda is bicarbonate of soda.
■ Vanilla is vanilla essence.
■ Green, red, or yellow sweet peppers are capsicums.
■ Golden raisins are sultanas.

Volume and Weight: Americans traditionally use cup measures for liquid and solid ingredients. The chart, below, shows the approximate imperial and metric equivalents. If you are accustomed to weighing solid ingredients, the following approximate equivalents will be helpful.
■ 1 cup butter, castor sugar, or rice = 8 ounces = about 250 grams
■ 1 cup flour = 4 ounces = about 125 grams
■ 1 cup icing sugar = 5 ounces = about 150 grams
  Spoon measures are used for smaller amounts of ingredients. Although the size of the tablespoon varies slightly in different countries, for practical purposes and for recipes in this book, a straight substitution is all that's necessary.
  Measurements made using cups or spoons always should be level unless stated otherwise.

Equivalents: U.S. = Australia/U.K.

⅛ teaspoon = 0.5 ml
¼ teaspoon = 1 ml
½ teaspoon = 2 ml
1 teaspoon = 5 ml
1 tablespoon = 1 tablespoon
¼ cup = 2 tablespoons = 2 fluid ounces = 60 ml
⅓ cup = ¼ cup = 3 fluid ounces = 90 ml
½ cup = ⅓ cup = 4 fluid ounces = 120 ml
⅔ cup = ½ cup = 5 fluid ounces = 150 ml
¾ cup = ⅔ cup = 6 fluid ounces = 180 ml
1 cup = ¾ cup = 8 fluid ounces = 240 ml
1¼ cups = 1 cup
2 cups = 1 pint
1 quart = 1 liter
½ inch =1.27 cm
1 inch = 2.54 cm

Baking Pan Sizes

American	Metric
8×1½-inch round baking pan	20×4-cm cake tin
9×1½-inch round baking pan	23×3.5-cm cake tin
11×7×1½-inch baking pan	28×18×4-cm baking tin
13×9×2-inch baking pan	30×20×3-cm baking tin
2-quart rectangular baking dish	30×20×3-cm baking tin
15×10×1-inch baking pan	30×25×2-cm baking tin (Swiss roll tin)
9-inch pie plate	22×4- or 23×4-cm pie plate
7- or 8-inch springform pan	18- or 20-cm springform or loose-bottom cake tin
9×5×3-inch loaf pan	23×13×7-cm or 2-pound narrow loaf tin or pâté tin
1½-quart casserole	1.5-liter casserole
2-quart casserole	2-liter casserole

Oven Temperature Equivalents

Fahrenheit Setting	Celsius Setting*	Gas Setting
300°F	150°C	Gas Mark 2 (slow)
325°F	160°C	Gas Mark 3 (moderately slow)
350°F	180°C	Gas Mark 4 (moderate)
375°F	190°C	Gas Mark 5 (moderately hot)
400°F	200°C	Gas Mark 6 (hot)
425°F	220°C	Gas Mark 7
450°F	230°C	Gas Mark 8 (very hot)
Broil		Grill

*Electric and gas ovens may be calibrated using Celsius. However, for an electric oven, increase the Celsius setting 10 to 20 degrees when cooking above 160°C. For convection or forced-air ovens (gas or electric), lower the temperature setting 10°C when cooking at all heat levels.